Broken
Wide
Whole

Prayers for Daily Living

by suzanne l. vinson

xo.
suzannelvinson

Broken Wide Whole: Prayers for Daily Living

Graphic design by Llewellyn Hensley / Content-Aware Graphic Design

First Printing, 2018
ISBN 978–0–692–15105–1

contents

about Broken Wide Whole

Today I arrive here to a planted field of hopes and dreams.
A fertile fields in which years of nurturing and preparing
the soil allows the rich bounty forth. Flowering words and
wilted words. Weedy thoughts. Dormant half-spoken words.
Seeds ripened and ready.

My journey to cultivate wholeness and integration found its
way through these words. I have lived these pages of prayers.
I had a place to grow. Each gave me something needed,
something necessary to living my days. Some prayers ushered
release while others echoed love.

My hope for this book is that it can be shared and used
as you have need. I know some aspect of this work will be
needed for those who feel pulled toward its pages — both
words and art. I know others will receive it because they were
thought of when the book was seen or held…may the words
be just what you need. Receive only what is welcome.

Know what is yours to carry and hold, and what is not.
I pray to loosen any bonds of pain that cause harm.
I pray for you. I pray for me. I pray for us.

Because I am created and have become more whole through
writing this work — it has reached its place of wholeness.
My prayer for these pages you hold is that they sing to your
soul, provide healing balm, and awaken you. May it be so.

suzanne l. vinson

Broken Wide Whole felt like it was whispered from the deepest part of my being. Suzanne creates a conduit between the reader and the holy, connecting the two through the beauty of language and art. Her gentle, compassionate and intimate language seem to translate messages from my own soul. Her words are embedded in the garden of her artwork, like they are each a prayer blooming from the soil. *Broken Wide Whole* is a book that can be revisited again and again, the prayers and conversations taking on newer and deeper meanings with each read. This book instructs the reader how to have her own intimate conversation with God.

— Valley Haggard, author of *The Halfway House for Writers* and *Surrender Your Weapons: Writing to Heal* and curator of lifein10minutes.com

A deep yes to suzanne l. vinson's *Broken Wide Whole*. Her profound words and whimsical art are a wake-up call for the spirit and a balm for the heart. In the exhale of each prayer is the vibration of compassion — for self, for other, for the human condition. suzanne shows us how to hold the pain and the joy of living as she embraces the mystery of each moment, each unfolding of truth. She invites us to let go, let in, take action, and take rest… and she reminds us of the divinity that lives within, around, and beyond us. This book is a pure offering of hope, gratitude, and wonder… a treasure for the human journey.

— Nicki Peasley, Author of *Ellipsis*

1

A Manifesto for A Spiritual Life

I will awaken to the world — both the world
around me and the wider world.

I will express my love and concern through
care in my feelings, my thoughts, and my actions.

Through love, my heart will remain open.

Living with an open heart, I will gladly welcome
the stories and experiences of others.

I will be kind and loving to myself and I will encourage
this kindness and love to flow to those I encounter daily.

I will care for my spirit as I welcome wisdom,
guidance, and learning.

My life will be lived in this moment with perspective,
gratitude, verve, and hope.

When the spark within nudges, prods, whispers
or shouts, I will slow down and pay attention.

I will pray, strike sparks, light the flame,
and welcome the Holy.

2

Deep Yes.

Today I embody my Deep Yes.

3

For Ease of Being.

Enfold us with your love, Source of Light and Life.
Grant that we may find the space to be enfolded,
that we allow ourselves the space to say, "Yes" to your
inviting spirit. You welcome us into your life freely.
May we experience your welcome through love as
we love ourselves and love others.

May we find the beauty and light that lives within.

May we live our days loving, comforted, and at peace.

May each breath be a breath of love.

May we discover our ease of being.

May we be our truest selves, knowing who we are.

May we enfold one another as tribe,
offering care and support to one another.

May we experience our strength and resilience with ease.

4

For a lighter load.

My load is heavy,
so I lay it down.
Awakening anew this day,
my spirit welcomes play.

5

Morning Mind.

Dwell within me,
spirit of love.

Dwell within and surround me,
spirit of peace.

Dwell within and surround me,
spirit of enduring hope.

Mornings are filled with awareness.

As I wake, my inner life of dreaming edges into my
consciousness like a mystical mist.

The mysteries of my dreams may return as I sip
my morning cup.

Looking out, I see the sun moving atop the darkness.

As steam rises from my cup, thoughts and hopes
rise to the surface of my mind.

Dwell
Within
me

6

For endurance

God of enduring love, compassionate voice, fierce spirit, and unyielding hope: May the time with our companions be as warm as a hand stitched blanket, filled to the brim with love and substance. May our life together be welcoming, filled with listening and story, hope and promise. When we are filled with mistrust, dis-ease, or hurt, may the bonds of friendship and family bridge the space to forgiveness and fresh beginnings. May we balance our needs of trust and dis-trust, because we know not all are safe, not all have purity of heart.

May wisdom guide us through the spaces of trust and safety. May wisdom show the path of welcome. We know we are here together in this Earth home. We grow in mind, body, and spirit. We're all here. Help us to grow old together, nurturing one another toward wholeness and welcome. Help us to befriend the neighbor who is hurting, and pray with loving-kindness for those who show hate. Help us to believe in our sacred goodness. Help us to not be scared. Help us to know when our fright is a means of survival, and when our fright is harmful to our selves.

There is always space for love, God of enduring love. Encircle us with your creative, creating love. Love formed the world. Love created us from dust. Before we return to dust, help us to be loving creatures filled with compassion, empathy, generosity, endurance, hope, trust, and love.

Fill us as you would your morning cup, to the brim.
Fill us with life and vitality, stardust and spark.

May our life endure through pain and suffering into spaces
of peace and comfort. May you heal the wounds, broken
hearts, cells overtaking cells, and bodies in chronic pain. May
you strengthen the weak thoughts of worry into a hope-
filled resolve. May you enable our bodies to receive pleasure
and provide pleasure when welcomed.

God, I want to ask you to redirect those who cause harm,
the predators and the ignorant, the racist and the bigoted,
though I cannot. Cleanse the thoughts from my own mind
of "better than" and "other" and help us to see one another
as your created beings. Help us to re-write the harmful
narratives that have been passed down to us. Help us not be
so wed to the ancient words written in your sacred texts that
we lose the heart of Your Love. My own transgressions weigh
heavily. Moments when I could have, should have, would have
acted, spoken, or moved differently with more time to think
and less time to feel threatened. Transform our petty arguments
into opportunities for conversation and healing. Be with us as
we pray, call your name, and work with compassion to heal the
world our home.

Heal our bodily homes, our minds, and our hearts. Enable
us to move through the pain to wisdom and empathy. Aim
our hearts and minds toward our life together. Help us know
who to trust, where to put our energy, and how to break into
our wholeness.

Put the people on our path
whom we need for our tribe,
who together help us to be
our full selves, helping us
to become strengthened,
uplifted, and stitched together.
We need each other. Each
day more than the day before.
Help us awaken to our needs
and the needs of others.
Help us heal from the illusions
of our separateness and the
manipulative ignorance
around us.

Our souls need peace.
Our minds need peace.
Our bodies need peace.
Bring peace.
Bring justice.
Bring mercy.
Bring kindness.
Bring healing.
Bring Love.

Amen.

7

For Blessing.

May your morning cup fill you
with what you need to step into your day.

May each sip move into your body
alongside courage and strength, hope and joy.

May you inhabit the spaces of your day
carrying only what you need to carry.

May wonder and mystery greet you
with their welcome spirit.

8

For A Hand Full of Truths.

I keep folding together the stories believing that one day the story folds will make a beautiful paper dove that will sail down the river. I'll place it there in my last breath.

A truth I carry — we grieve as one.

Let me tell you a secret…I have decided to believe in myself.

I can tell you a thing or two about hope. Hope can ring in your ears. Hope can capture your heart. Hope can fill your lungs with abundance. Hope can fill your hands with truth.

9

For Being.

I am broken wide whole.

10

For Hope.

May those who live in broken spaces
find the healing that is needed.

May those who long for news receive good word.

May those who are hurting and helpless
be held in loving arms & receive blessing.

May healing be found, doors be opened,
& food be served. May families be reunited.

May stranger & guest share a meal together.

11

For Today.

Today I listen.
at the water's edge,
at the edge of containment and contentment.

Cicadas.
Water cascading.
The hymn of life all around.
The river moves and I move with it.
The breeze cools my fiery thoughts.
If I touch my pen to tongue the words will burn.

Today I am broken wide whole.
Again.
In my thousand mornings I've awakened to myself.
Sitting at the edge of containment and contentment,
Dis-ease and misunderstanding clamor for attention.

The cicadas win.
The river frog comes in a close second.
My heart leaps with the frog.
A welcome exclamation of exuberance.

Here. Here I am.
Exactly where I am meant to be in this moment.
Showing up to myself.
A steady commitment.

Today I am broken wide whole.
Resting in the comforts of flesh and bone.

12

For Living Whole.

To be broken wide whole, one must move from a place of
beauty into a place of beautiful mess. Your heart is tread on,
torn, wounded, or bruised. The traumas of your past resurface,
the wind is knocked out of your chest, and you wander in a
land of mystery and at times misery. For some, being broken
wide whole involves a shattering of the ego that for others
happened years before. For others, a break in a relationship of
the echo of relationships long ago pierced your heart. To be
broken wide whole, all your energy must turn inward to hold
all these pieces in place. You heal by turning trust to a few
and not spreading it thin. You heal in prayer and in solitude.
You heal in your spaces of worship — within walls and within
nature. You heal as you recognize the power and beauty you
carry in your broken wide wholeness. Being broken wide whole,
the Divine Spark that radiates within you shines even brighter
through the cracks. Your broken wide wholeness is a way of
becoming you that you would not have asked for, but give
thanks for. You know that you are more fully you, stronger and
more secure. Kinder and more compassionate to yourself and
to others through your gratitude for your life. The beautiful
mess has taught you to be more accepting of your instincts,
more attuned to listening and acting on wisdom, and to loving
who you're meant to love. To be broken wide whole, to live
in that wholeness, you're given a gentle strength to tend to
yourself.

Sometimes that tending extends to others as an extension of true love, where nothing is expected in return. You return to yourself, broken wide whole and lovingly tend to inner workings of your life. You return to the world, broken wide whole, with strength and innate beauty. The contents of your beautiful self spill out into the world through the calm energy you carry within. Your life and love extend to the world around you, and you are living whole.

Give thanks. Give thanks. Give thanks.

13

For Finding Meaning.

It's another what-does-my-life-mean kind of morning. My existential crisis before coffee. When PMS meets midlife passage, oh dear. Bless my heart. I just cannot decide what to do or where to go. So I meet the morning with coffee in hand. I make breakfast for my loves. I pack my lunch and prepare for another day of work. My hope is that the daily tasks move me closer to the heart of being. My questions have their place. Meaning will find its place. May mystery meet me with open arms this day. May wisdom dance with me. May my heart and mind and body have an ease of being. May I embrace wholeness — the unknowing, unknowable, and known. May this day be filled with all-that-is-life.

14

For Navigating the Fog.

God, help me to navigate the moments when I am ill-at-ease, when my intuition meets well-worn neural pathways of uncertainty. The Wellspring of Wisdom bubbles up, yet my old fearful thoughts intrude. My cupped hands reach into the well, and emerge with sand. I am clouded by my thoughts. I am unable to discern truth from false belief. My energy is circling the drain and I feel as though I could abandon hope. Help me navigate through this fog. Part the clouds and shine the light of truth. Help my cupped hands receive the water of wisdom I seek in pursuit of truth over false belief. Help me find my way to clarity, truth, and peace.

15

For Healing Circles.

We find each other. We who have been harmed by good intention. We who have been harmed by touch. We who have been harmed by abusive language. We who have been prey to those who seek to do harm. We bind our-selves to one another in a spirit of healing. Our spoken and unspoken stories go into a sacred trust.

We heal one another.

16

For Letting Go.

Sometimes when I think it's my task to do the healing work, it's really my task to let go and trust another to do their work. To weed the belief that it's mine to carry when it's not. I must not succumb to the mirage of peril, the chaos of the mind, the weakening belief that I alone am not enough, disruptive to time and space, that my presence requires apology. No, thank you.

All too easily I can tap into the shoulds and woulds and coulds of it all. I could become mired in those questions... but not today. Today I will call upon my resources, my intellect, and my life experience thus far to release from the belief that it's my work when it's my true task to let go.

17

For a Hurting Friend.

God, please help my friend find peace.
True peace, deep peace.
She's being broken wide whole.

Her heart is hurt but thankfully still beating.
Her life is upturned, messy, and mired,
and she is in such misery.

May her tears bring release.
May she release her fear of the unknown
and unknowable.
May she rest, even when sleepless.
May she feel beyond the stinging pain.

May the words over shared meals fill her with love.
May she delight in food again.
May she know her tribe loves her.
May she know she is still lovable. Always lovable.
So very lovable.

May she know that not all who surround her
are ready to do harm, even though harm exists
and has been all too present to her.

God, please enfold her with outstretched arms.
Kindly bring comfort to her,
offering her your healing balm.

May your love and comfort and true peace,
deep peace, reach each cell in her body.
May she know her wholeness.

18

For You.

You are you.
The you you are created to be,
the you you are becoming.
You are infinite and vast.
You are singular and whole.
Your completeness is unfolding before you.
As you age, you become more distinctly you.
Your beauty is a gradual becoming.
A sunrise and sunset of loveliness.
You are you, loving one.
You are beautiful and whole. Spirit and body.

You are you in this moment and the next.
You are dressed in love.
Your light invites others near, like a moth to the lamp.

19

For Us.

Let us not fade from each other's vision.
Let us not become unknown to one another.

BE you. BE light.

20

For a Feast.

Before the bread
    there was the wheat.
Before the wheat
    there was the stalk.
Before the stalk
    there was the seed.
Before the seed
    there was fertile soil.
Before fertile soil
    there was the space.
There with the space were willing hands.

21

For Reading Between the Lines.

Between the lines on paper are frown lines and worry lines. Lines being drawn in the sand, walls going up, and threats that weaken my sanity. We must remember that people are people. Love is love. We're each created for this time, yet some draw lines to separate "some" from "other" from "good" from "better" from "weak" from "bad"... so much of our time will be devoted to the work that lies ahead.

Perhaps we forget to say "I'm sorry" but instead say, "I'm of more value than you." If I convince myself I am of that sort of value, I might feel valued. In truth, my worry lines say I am forgetting how to love myself, so it makes sense I'm not sure how to practice loving you.

22

For Opening Lines of Communication.

We can share more, and sometimes too much,
through the instant spread of information.

Lines are crossed that shouldn't be crossed.
Our moral compass is ignored, perhaps from weak use.

We sink into the mire of our collective depression.
Our hearts are heavy and we lack clarity.

We slink into holes and hide ourselves.
We lack the energy to make authentic connections.

Our voices keep silent.
It's long past time to invite folks into conversation.

23

For my Deep Yes.

The entrapments of the past
become memories that have lost their glisten.

I listen to my inner knowing
and say YES to this moment.

From the Deep Yes within,
my soul shines and I find my voice.

I ask for what I need
and new neural pathways form.

I receive the blessing of YES
and respond with thanks.

My soul deepens and widens.

24

For Enduring Love and Light.

God of the {enduring} morning, grant me peace this day.
Grant that I may listen to only the voices who have earned
hearing. Grant that the energy that flows into my body is
the energy that endures. Grant that my breath be filled with
your goodness and mercy.

For the early days hearing unkind words, may their echo be
reduced to memory. For the unkind touches and advances on
my body, may there no longer be muscle memory but strength.
For the moments of true love and compassion, may they be felt
on the surface of memory and deep within. For the pure joy
and delight that moves into my being, may they be received
and welcomed.

God of enduring hope and promise, you know my habits and
my longings. You know when I rest and when I rise. You know
when I fall to the abuses of the world around me, when I become
sucked into the energy flow of anxiety, mistrust, and abuse. You
know when my heart is laughing and when I know complete
despair.

God of light, my heart radiates love and energy, and I learn
from my mistakes. I learn when to rise and when to rest.
I know when to hold onto hope and when to release unrealized
dreams. I ask the questions of my heart and mind and seek
answers in mystery.

My comfort comes in welcoming the stranger within, as I unfold within a busy, bustling world. My world is constructed of gathered objects, places, and people who help my heart to laugh and to sing. Music fills my days and I learn to dance the dance of wisdom and courage and healing.

With resilience and radiance, I welcome this new day. With understanding and mystery, I dance with the unknown and speak with a clear voice. My bruised ego heals. My failings fall to the ground. I am welcomed as I welcome. I find peace as I live peace. My life endures pain and suffering as I awaken to the pain and suffering of others. May we create habits and longings that fill us up with Your Radiant Love. May your enduring light become brighter as we return to you our energy, light, and life.

Amen.

25

For Peace with Each Breath

I want to have peace in each breath, but the air I'm breathing feels stifled by anxiety. The undercurrent of scarcity is stifling. I cannot breathe. IF I cannot breathe, I cannot use my voice. Help us to treat each other with respect and authenticity. Let us BE creation. Be ourselves with other people. Be people of infinite possibility. People who love with each breath and word and step. People of infinite love and hope, filled with life. In this dream, we're hand in hand traversing the love-populated streets where we are created to be love and share love freely. Where love isn't judged but rather lived whole with freedom and promise.

With peace
in each breath,
let us travel
our landscapes
of love, hope,
and promise.

26

For release.

My belly hurts. Once again foods have unseated me.
My stomach gurgles and sings and causes discomfort.
I know what is good for me and what is not good for me.
Much like the food that enters my body, there are times
when I consume the energy of others that is not good for me.
My belly hurts then, too. It's difficult to judge what's what
until a day later. It's an effort to keep calm and be at peace.
Only it's in the days that follow that my belly speaks.
So I let go, literally and emotionally.
I release and free myself once again.

27

For Sprouting Hope.

Let us create spaces of healing, trust, and beauty.

Let us gather the Sacred Other near
and speak in compassionate tones.

Let us be present to the field of wildflowers
growing within, sprouting hope and love, peace and joy.

28

For Light.

Spirit of truth, speak to us through wisdom's light.
Spirit of play, speak through your twinkling stars.
Spirit of rest, speak through the dawning light.
Spirit of desire, speak through candle lit spaces.
Spirit of hope, speak through Your Light.

29

For Clear Paths.

I cannot help but find hope
in the what is and what will be.
We are created for this moment,
and we are here.

Because we are here,
we must operate in ways of truth and justice,
inhabiting holy spaces of extraordinary beauty
and traveling sacred paths of rest.

30

For Illumination.

Illuminate my spark.
Illuminate the joy within.
As the sun strikes the glittering beauty of the
newly fallen snow, illuminate what my spirit holds.

Illuminate the beauty I forget to see.
Illuminate the beauty I forget to feel.
Speak in your hidden truths and
not-so-hidden blessings that sparkle.

With moon light, illuminate the beauty within that is only
seen in the nighttime darkness. The fertile ground brims with
life. Spirit of living presence, you are joined to me through
the life-force brimming within. Your eternal presence is a
thread that connects all. You embody truth, light, and love.
Our journey is to you. Our path is ever fixed in the here and
now. The I that I'm becoming. Illuminate the words that carry
me closer to your rightness, your life force, your rootedness.
I seek guidance, wisdom, truth. I reject what separates us
from you and from one another.

31

With a Full Heart.

With a thankfull heart, we give thanks.
With a joyful heart, we sing.
With a loving heart, we sow love.
With a gracious heart, we sit beside.
With a grateful heart, we breathe.

32

For the What If?

What if we lived like black lives matter?
What if all lives truly mattered?

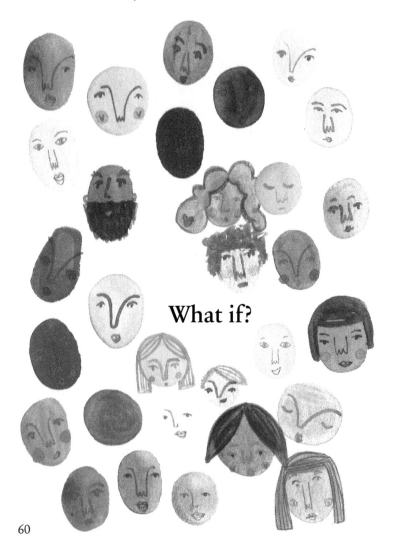

What if?

33

For Hope Renewed.

God of enduring hope, God of radical hope and promise.
You make yourself known to us, filling us with love and life
and abundance. Heal our broken hearts. Grant us courage
in the light of hope-less-ness. You are our source of life and
light and inspiration and trust. Help us to endure hardship,
disappointment, and heartache for the sake of love. Help us
to be strengthened in faith and learning. Make our hearts
whole, our lives meaningful, and our integrity unbroken.
Bind us to the love that created us. Make us yours as you
made us. May our lives be filled with welcome and the promise
for hope renewed. Give us the gift of your light and love. Fill
us with your grace. Explore our hearts to the pursuit of
justice in love. May we be faithful stewards of your love, hope,
and promise.

Amen.

34

For Grief.

The time to grieve is upon you.

Grief's grip follows you in your sleep and into dreams.

Every fiber of your being is touched.
Your tears flow as memories rise to the surface.

In each breath,
may a moment of peace move into your body.

May that peace grow into wider stretches where
comfort, healing, and rest abound.

May you know that the ebb and flow of loss stretch
you and bring healing to all the weary spaces.

...

Just as there is no measure for love,
there is no measure for loss.

As your heart breaks and finds its way to mending —
May you heal from the depth of your belonging.
May you know you are not alone.
May each day add comfort, peace, and pause.
May memories be welcome and hold love.
May love encircle you and flow through you.
May eat, sleep, and daily rhythms bring you
closer to mourning.

Peace be with you.
Deep Peace be with you.

35

For an Open Heart.

We are called to remember. We are rememberers.

May memories come in a gentle flow.

May your memories and your tears be instruments
of healing and love.

May love surround you just as the cloud of witnesses
surrounds you and your community.

May you find blessing in memory, release in letting go,
and the space to love with an open heart.

36

For Memory.

May the echo of memory serve you well.

May distortions and questions become
refined words of hope and healing.

May your memories be like blooms that
serve you in love, flowering into new life.

37

For Rest and Recovery.

May this moment be a blessing to you.

As you rest and recover, may you find healing and hope.

May each breath come with ease.

May each moment be filled with calm and care.

May your heart and your mind and your body
find the resilience and truth of healing.

As you breathe, may each fiber of your being be healed.

May the light shine upon you, bringing warmth and wonder.

38

For Focus.

As you tend the tasks of this day,
may your mind recall all your preparation.

May anxieties lessen as you find your inner calm.

May your belly be full and your posture straight.

May you walk with a confident trust in yourself.

May the night's sleep bring true rest upon a job
earnestly done.

39

For Beginnings.

As you are called to new beginnings.

As you begin anew, may you be encircled by love.

May joy fill you all the way to your toes.

May peace be in each breath.

May hope give you wings to soar.

May your wholeness be met in the light and beauty of this season of love, hope, peace, and joy.

40

For Being Light.

Help us to BE light.
Help us to delight in being light.

41

For Healing.

May you know you are not alone.

You are surrounded by light and love.

Welcome thoughts and memories that give life
and energy as you release pain and discomfort.

May you know your presence in this world
as a gift of worth and value.

May you encounter beauty in and around you,
providing space for gratitude and delight.

May you find comfort and peace in each moment.

May each breath bring you hope.

42

With a Welcome Heart.

With a welcome heart, I shine.
With a shining heart, I sing.
With a loving heart, I grow.
With a growing heart, I dance.
With a dancing heart, I delight.

43

For Receiving Support.

Breathe in and out love,
ushering in a sense of calm.

Accept peace through wholeness and trust.

Take refuge in safe spaces
and embody wholeness, life, and light.

May you offer a holy welcome
to those who support you.

May sacred space be found
and filled with the holy.

May you find your tribe and gather near
those who are kind, loving, brave, and true.

44

For Knowing What to Carry

May we know our Deep Peace.
May we know our Deep Yes.
May we know our Deep Ease.
May we know our Deep Delight.

May we carry our Deep Peace.
May we carry our Deep Yes.
May we carry our Deep Ease.
May we carry our Deep Delight.

45

For Goodness.

There is so much goodness brimming from within.
Dive into the waters
of your life
...and swim.

46

For Praying with My Littles.

Loving God, Thank you for this life.
Thank you for love.
Thank you for home and family and making me.
Thank you for a voice to sing and talk and pray.
Thank you for feet to dance and run and skip.
Thank you for helpers and friends.
Thank you for my church and my school.
Thank you for...

Amen.

47

For Praying with My Littles at Night.

Thank you for this day.
Thank you for this world
and everything in it.

Thank you for the moon
and the sun, for the stars
and the sky.

Thank you for food,
and water, and love,
and for making each
so very special.

Amen.

48

For a New Family.

Creator of Life, who breathes us into being, whose spirit is our
first breath, whose knowing is our first knowing... grant your
spirit of love, presence, and peace. Surround parents who birth
hope today. To parents whose child comes from birthing waters
into this world full of infinite possibility, draw your loving
presence near. As you draw near, dance among these, pouring
all the love and affection coming from many parts of creation
to those we love and bless.

Well-maker, bless the wellspring whose waters flow forth:
tears of love, tears of gratitude, tears of pain, tears of joy, tears
with no name. These waters from your source become waters
of welcome, as part of the birthing waters this day.

Creative Presence, as you have paired creatively these who
will love and be loved, may your spirit work within the trans-
formation taking place through love. Whether by labor of love
in a car, train, and plane to birth a new babe who arrives
through hopes and dreams and love in a creative, courageous
way, or through the process of labor, birthing a child in a
room with midwife and parent, soothe and support their
laboring love.

Wellspring of Life, may the anticipation of waiting and watching and laboring become the sacred gift of life, the gift of hope, the gift of dream. Bless these who wait, these who welcome, these whose hearts are filled so full. Bless the prayers and hopes and dreams surrounding creative mystery this day.

Mothering God, may birth bring pure love, light and peace to these and their supportive families and friends. Delight be shared in all ways on this day and the days to come for these parents who travel to meet their child and for children who travel to meet their parents. May birthing waters within, and oceans, be waters that bring miracles for this new family.

Amen.

49

For Your Hands and Mine.

Yours are the hands I hold.
The hands I rub lotion onto.
The hands I wash, the hands I dry.
Yours are the hands that are folded in prayer.
The hands that know my touch.
The hands that greet me and the hands that wave good bye.

My hands are the hands I hold.
My hands greet your hands with gentleness and love.
My hands are worn and dry from a hundred washings a day.
My hands are now in the gentle care of your touch.

When my hands work for yours,
when you cannot brush your teeth or eat your meal,
my hands are hands that bring nourishment and health.

May your hands be blessed.
May your hands be cared for the way you show care
to others. Your hands are a blessing unto others.

50

A Word Liturgy.

refuge
find your refuge in safe spaces of comfort
and trust.

comfort
find comfort in your own skin.

awaken
awaken to the love that lives within and
surrounds you.

plant
be rooted in fertile spaces and give yourself
room to grow.

seek
live your adventure with open eyes and
an open heart.

tend
cultivate love and wholeness with tender
hands and heart.

explore
embody spaces of gratitude and wholeness.

wonder
open to the Deep Yes and sparkling warmth
of wonder.

show up
be your beautiful best, fully present to
who you are and who you are becoming.

share
spread joy, love, and hope as you share your story.

encircle
gather your tribe and enrich one another's lives
with tender beauty.

dwell
live a life you love. love the life you live.
be well within.

For the Widening Circle.

What began as a seed took root and became something beautiful. For those who tended the fertile fields of this work, I give thanks.

I give thanks for my love, Richard, and my littles, Joseph and Cora Rose whose love and encouragement is unending. You give my daily living a deeper purpose and allow my art to take the best forms possible.

I give thanks for my circle of women who surround me close, for Jayme Reaves, Courtney E. Allen, Erin Spenge Hutchison, Patience Salgado as early readers and responders whose early edits, comments, and gentle nudges were invaluable.

For Nicki Peasley and her energy healing pouring through me — your energy and healing flowed through these words, too, love. Thank you for holding this work close and keeping a close eye on grammar that might interrupt the flow of energy and healing for each who read.

Valley Haggard, wise woman and kindred spirit, I give thanks for you and the timing of our meeting — you were my writing midwife and coach and gave me the footing to put the words written over the past few years into the space of this book. Thank you for seeing the title before I did.

I give thanks for you, Llewellyn Hensley, and the mighty way your graphic design elevates this work. Thank you for your time and energy and skills integrated within.

I give thanks for Elizabeth Thalhimer Smartt and her hard edits of the final body of this work — you have strengthened my words and presence in the world.

For Annie Campbell, Amanda Fall, Casey Freeman, Phoebe Guider, Elizabeth M. Lott, Nikole Sarvay, my wider family, and my Creativity Circle folks who received prayers and responded along the way. Each of you give me grounding and love. Thank you. Thank you. Thank you.

We are never alone, and I give thanks for the ever widening circles of support, love, and generosity that flow through you here. Thank you for welcoming my words and art into daily living.

Light. Peace.
suzanne l. vinson